The Well of True Gestures

When Love FINDS YOU

Stephanie Roberts

ISBN: 978-0-6485363-3-8

Stephanie Roberts/Author Wyoming, Gosford, NSW 2250

https://www.facebook.com/StephanieRobertsAuthor/

https://stephaniemarieroberts.com

The Well of True Gestures

To Help Couples Bond in their Relationship

The true romantic things in life are those little things you do every day to show you care, and that you are thinking of your significant other. Romance isn't about buying, it's about giving.

True Romance is in the Gestures.

Each heart-card is co-ordinated with the colour of the chakra energy.

Feel the connection. Build trust. Be there for one another. Make time for each other. Appreciate the flaws. Appreciate each other. Become best friends.

Love Each Other Unconditionally.

Pick a heart-card each day at random, or of your choice, together with your partner, for 28 days. Make the effort. See your relationship change and grow.

Definitely.

COMMUNICATE
WITH EACH
OTHER

Without communication, a relationship will die. It is as necessary as oxygen is to life.

Try to listen to **UNDERSTAND** first before **REPLYING.**

A false or misunderstood word may create as much disaster as a thoughtless act.

A Great Relationship has Great Communication.

Express yourself effectively and clearly. Listen properly to your significant other.

Communication is a skill that can be learned. Like riding a bicycle.

The most important thing in communication is hearing what isn't being said. It's the art of

reading between the lines.

Communication is the Human Connection.

What things bring you happiness and feelings of connection?

What things cause you disappointment and pain?

GIVE EACH OTHER A MASSAGE

Couples can improve their wellbeing by giving each other a massage.

A couples massage encourages bonding. Massage stimulates the release of many feel-good hormones, which boost feelings of intimacy and affection. It relaxes the body, soothes the mind and revives the soul.

So basically, a couples massage is pretty much a scientific love potion!

Massages stop short of orgasm (or at least they're supposed to), leaving you hovering on the brink and ready for your lover to complete the act …

Give each other

A Happy Ending Massage!

PLAY MAID
FOR THE
DAY

Men love to be spoilt and given special attention.

Boys and their toys! Why not play some PlayStation or Xbox with your man for a night?

Be your partner's Maid for a Day. Treat your partner like royalty for a day. Or even a few

hours, if your partner doesn't allow you to play the maid for an entire day.

You can even wear a French maid's dress!

Give him a shave. Lay out his clothes.

Bring him a glass of beer/wine. Prepare him snacks and watch the game with him,

cheering

on his favourite player and team. Grab that joystick and give him a little competition on the

X-box or PlayStation.

Serve him a special meal (while you tease him with the feather duster).

No dessert. Tell him … you are the dessert. Tie a red ribbon

with a bow around yourself.

Come on … I'm sure you can think of something.

HOT

COOK TOGETHER

Cooking is an activity that allows a couple to connect on an intimate level, to be creative and strengthen their relationship.

Cooking well doesn't mean cooking fancy. The secret ingredient is always Love. Cooking is love made visible.

No matter how you slice and dice it, food and love are inextricably tied. Culinary skills are sexy. Learn together.

Great food is like great sex. The more you have the more you want.

Sexay.

Help your partner prepare dinner and wash the dishes.

Wear nothing but aprons!

Maybe a little food fight?

Think of something innovative.

Don't forget the candles and Pinot Grigio.

WRITE A LOVE
LETTER TO EACH
OTHER

Texting is the norm in our day of technology. But it still can't measure up to the impact of a handwritten love letter.

What can you say in a love letter that won't come across as too mushy or too clichéd? LOTS, and you don't have to be a skilled writer to write words that will touch each other's hearts.

Show your love and effort by going another step. Pick a perfect bouquet of roses and place your love letter in it, or prepare your lover's favourite meal and place the letter in an envelope along with the dessert.

Start strong. Go right to what matters most.

Be specific. Zero in on each other's most outstanding traits.

Make an impact statement. Write about the difference he has made in your life. If he's the rock you depend on, give an example of a time that was evident.

Talk about the special moments you've shared together and how much they mean to you.

Write about anything that you strongly feel and appreciate about your lover.

DATE NIGHT IN

If you have kids your date starts once they go to bed. Stay-in dates don't require a lot of time and money but can make a big impact in helping you to reconnect with your partner.

Get creative and come up with a fun one-on-one activity you can do with your partner without leaving the house.

Eat take-out by candlelight with a bottle of wine. Make time to talk. Put on your favourite music. Dance cheek-to-cheek, or rock-n-roll!

Lay out a blanket in your backyard, set out a lantern, and eat dinner or dessert under the stars.

Baby monitors are long-range these days so you can keep check on your little one.

Get romantic by lighting some candles and soaking in a relaxing bubble bath with your lady love.

Make a bucket list of all the travel and micro adventures you would like to do together.

A little friendly competition can set the sparks flying again—bring out a board game!

REMINISCENCE

Reminiscing about the 'way we were' can revive your relationship. As you trigger a memory of an experience you had with your significant other, you strike a responsive chord and some of those old feelings come back.

Taking a trip down memory lane helps to fortify and renew your relationship.

Get out old photos or videos and relive those memories from your past. Play music from that era or from an event itself, such as your wedding.

Laugh together when recalling things that didn't go as planned.

Indulge in enjoyable recollection of past events.

Talk about special moments, the things that first attracted you to each other.

Reminisce about sweet memories, such as the birth of a child. The marriage proposal. How did you know I was the one you wanted to marry?

Reminiscence about your Love Story.

EXPRESS
APPRECIATION

Appreciate what you have, where you are and who you are with in this moment. Appreciation can make your partner's day and bring you closer. Simply put it into words.

It's easy to slip into the habit of taking each other for granted and stop caring for and appreciating each other. This can lead to arguments, frustration, resentment and suddenly wondering if the relationship is meant to work out. Healthy relationships keep evolving. When it comes to love, appreciating your partner is never enough. Make appreciating your partner a priority to keep the spark alive. Appreciate them for who they truly are as a person.

Acknowledge what you love about your partner, their family or their friends. Compliment them on simple things you love about them. For example, say something nice about their optimism, their strength, their kindness or their hard work.

Let them know how much you are attracted to them. It's always nice for your partner to know you still find them.

♥ Sexy.

FIX THINGS
TOGETHER

When Love FINDS YOU

Not every decision in a healthy household needs to be a consensus agreement. Part of being in a relationship is knowing where your strengths complement the other person's weaknesses.

Doing things together is easier than arguing about whose job it should be.

Decide to fix at least three small things today—and get the job done!

What needs fixing around your house?

A leaky faucet—only usually needs a new washer. Save the water bill.

That cupboard door with a loose hinge that drives her mad.

That loose doorknob that keeps coming off. Annoying!

She wanted a feature wall bright blue, remember. Paint it. Together.

She's been asking for those brass handles on the buffet … for how long?

Get them today!

Re-caulk the damaged old caulking around the bathtub and

shower to look fresh with bright white new caulking.

What needs doing in your house?

Get that paint, hammer and screwdriver out now!

Remember the time to fix the roof is when the sun is shining …

When Love Finds You

FORGIVE TODAY

Forgiveness is a bold step in the right direction.

Forgiving your partner if they've done something to upset you can be one of the hardest things to do in a relationship. It can be more tempting to hang on to negative emotions. You act distant and frosty as a way of punishing the person who has upset you. When you feel disappointed, angry or betrayed, the thought of forgiving your partner can feel like giving in—as if by letting go of your resentment, you're allowing them to 'get away with it'.

A beautiful relationship does not depend on how well we understand someone. It depends on how well we avoid misunderstanding. It helps you both move forward together.

Are you harbouring a grudge?

Let go of your anger and let go of the 'moral high ground'. Consider how you may have contributed to the argument. Although it's tempting to imagine oneself as completely in the right when it comes to disagreements, there are usually two sides to any argument.

Talk to your partner—be vulnerable.

Heal and forgive each other.

Reaffirm all the things that each has done right. Problems occur because each is concentrating on what is missing in the other partner.

SPEND 15 MINUTES CONNECTING

Love FINDS YOU

Every relationship encounters disagreements or conflict at times. But when we have a secure emotional connection with our loved one this is only a temporary feeling and nonthreatening. For those who have a weaker emotional connection, the fear can feel devastating, leaving some with a sense of panic. These feelings often occur on an unconscious level. It is not until we bring them into our awareness that things can begin to change.

Our loved one should be a source of comfort, security and refuge. When life gets full of things like growing careers, rearing children, balancing home life and work, our emotional connection can become compromised.

Start by appreciating something about each other. Him: 'Aside from food, you're my favourite.'

Her: 'I'm always amazed at the things you don't find embarrassing about me.'

Offer some new information from your day—'Our Jenny, 9 going on 17, wants to leave school and jump to college. She says she's bored with school.'

Tell your spouse something about yourself—'I'd like to learn karate; in case someone jumps me after my gym class.'

Silly. But you get it. Put your spin on it.

Connect.

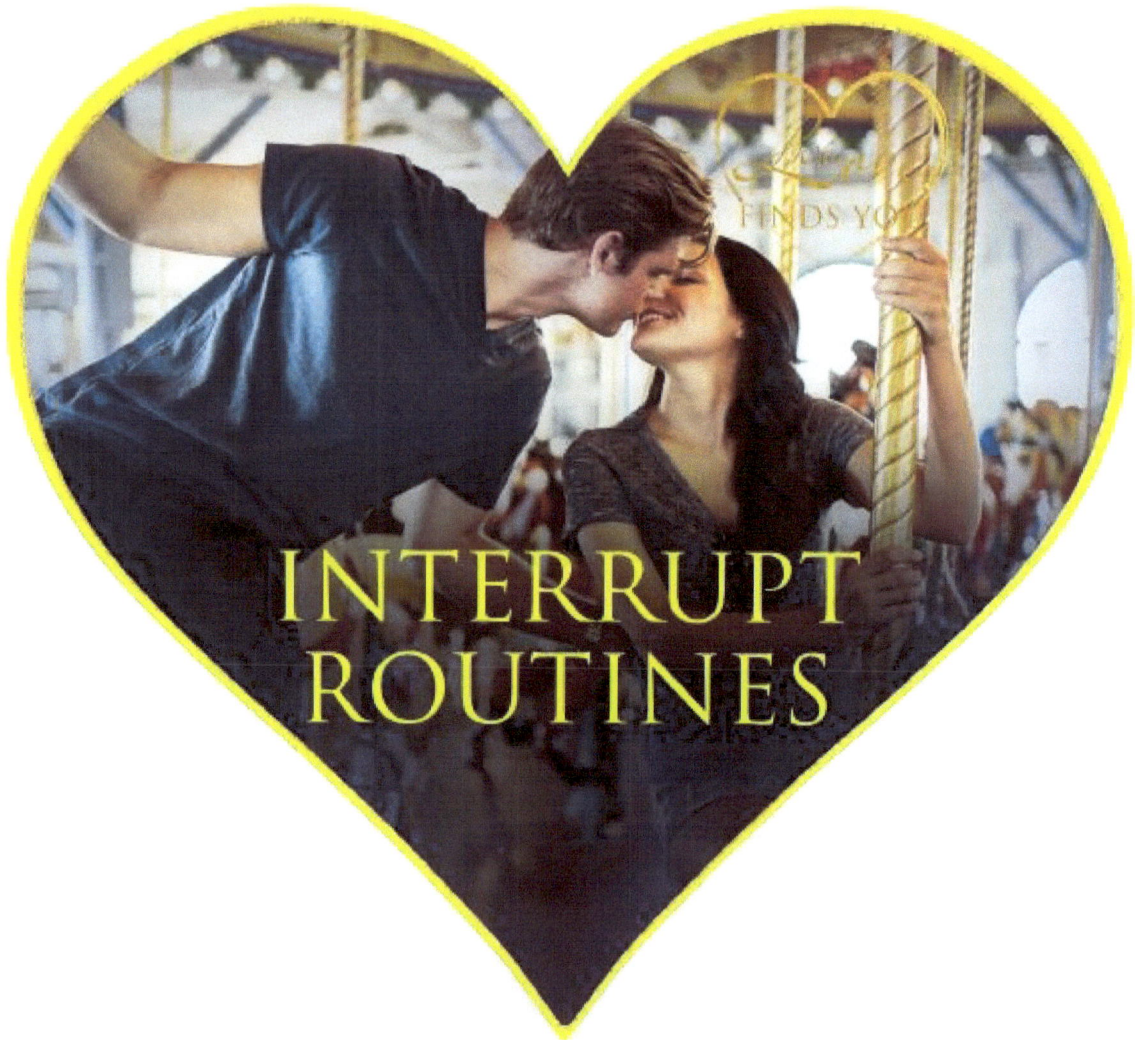

INTERRUPT
ROUTINES

A relationship is a living thing that needs nourishment to grow. Fertilise it like a plant and introduce change into your relationship. Variation from the everyday routine is important to make things more fun.

While it is wonderful to get away to some exotic island where you both could spend days sipping Pina Coladas on the beach, it is good to have some ways to electrify your relationship during normal everyday life.

Check out a new neighbourhood together and visit the coffee shop and arty places. Explore your next town.

She usually goes to her type of shows and you go out with the boys. Buy tickets to a show of your choice (on different nights!) and accompany each other to the concert of your choice. Both parties get to hear their favourites and it gives the other insights about their partner.

Stargaze at night. Name your stars. Sitting together under the moon and stars is simple and romantic, with a glass of wine or cup of coffee.

Hit an amusement park and bring some childlike fun back into your life.

There's zero reason not to go to an amusement park when you're an adult.

He loves playing pool. You love painting. Teach each other your favourite hobby. Teaching and learning together brings you much closer. Be patient and idiotic with each other.

GET PHYSICAL

Have Sex! No excuse needed! One of the biggest reasons why physical intimacy is important in a relationship is because this is one of the foremost ways in which partners express their love for one another.

When a relationship lacks sexual chemistry and physical affection it is likely to fail.

Are you both bored of your bedroom antics and fancy

spicing things up between the sheets?

Try these 12 tantric sex positions if you're

sick of missionary. Which ones will you

be brave enough to try?

SHOW
GENEROSITY
TODAY

Turbocharge your relationship with the high-octane fuel called Generosity. Thoughtful little gestures go a long way in love. Giving oneself fully in relationship is the ultimate gift.

Pick up her favorite snack on the way home. It's a small gesture, but one that shows you were thinking of your significant other.

Say 'Thank you'. For the little things and the bigger ones.

Give a gift. For no occasion. Or that puppy she is longing for? That's real generous.

Forgive. For that one thing you were still holding against him.

Breakfast in bed. Get up earlier and make your partner breakfast in bed. Or coffee and toast. Who wouldn't appreciate that? Can't go wrong.

Make a list of things you love about your partner and share it with them.

– I trust you –

– I'm on your side –

– You always know how to make me smile –

– I've never felt safer and more comfortable around anyone else –

– I've never been more turned on by anyone –

– You make me weak in the knees so often –

– I'm proud of you –

I'm sure you have your special loving thoughts.

TAKE
A COUPLE
CLASS

Love
FINDS YOU

Doing the exact same things can get boring, so it's in your best interest to do new things with your partner, which will enhance your relationship. Grab your partner's hand and go to these artsy, helpful and sexy couple classes for a sweet and fun relationship.

Take a Massage Class together. It just might put you in the mood for some frisky fun too!

Express yourself in Acting Class.

Mix a cocktail in Mixology Class. Discover tasty drink recipes and impress your friends with professionalquality cocktails.

Shake it in Dance Class. She likes to dance, even if you don't. Think about how much fun she would have in a swing, tango, or ballroom dancing class.

Kama Sutra Class. Who wouldn't like to have a more explosive and pleasurable sex life with their partner?

There is nothing wrong with wanting to improve intimacy with a person you love and care about very much. Kama Sutra class will teach you new ways to explore your partner's body that you never thought of before and will help you become more comfortable with communicating your desires in bed.

INTERRELATEDNESS

Interrelatedness. An unfamiliar word. It's about keeping your partner up-to-date on the small things you think, see, and experience. It is a wonderful fun connection when you are away from each other during the day. The minutiae of everyday life.

Shoot them an email about your colleague's wacky tie.

A swimming pig with a passenger on his head. Really?

Send them a Snapchat pic of any random, meaningless and mundane funny things that you notice throughout the day. Granddad is mowing the lawn in his underwear, the neighbour's three-year-old kid is filling up his mother's petrol tank with the water hose. Text them about the annoying colleagues sitting on either side of your desk. Mark is obsessively clicking pens and James is chewing gum like a cow munching on grass. Arrrgh! Text them some juicy office gossip. Jenny is making eyes at the boss and her skirt is above her thighs … Make sure the boss doesn't have a look over your shoulder.

And someone stole my lunch from the refrigerator.

The silly stuff. But it's a warm fuzzy feeling to interrelate.

DOUBLE
DATE

Call up your closest couple friends and get that date on the calendar, stat.

If you and your partner have been together a long time, a double date is a fun way to switch up your time together. Whether the double date is with your significant other's friends, yours, or your mutual friends, spending time with other couples can shake up your regular date night.

It's a fun way to do something different.

Couples who chat about personal topics with others say they feel more in love with each other after than those who just engage in small talk.

What's something that a lot of people are afraid of, but you aren't?

What's the biggest financial mistake you've made?

What was the hardest lesson you've had to learn?

What do you worry about?

Suggestions. They are your closest couple friends. Add your own.

Make sure your double date involves a lot of warm and personal conversation.

Dinner and drink—good.

Movies or loud concert—bad.

SURPRISE
EACH
OTHER

Keeping romance alive isn't a walk in the park.

Small surprises can make a big impact.

Go Old School with a romantic candlelit dinner. If you can't cook, order take-out. Candlelight is romantic and intimate.

Throw your significant other an Un-Birthday Party. Any sort of fun party or BBQ, where they are the guest of honour, with their family/friends. Make a loving speech to tell them how special they are.

Re-create your first date. Show your partner how much you care with a trip down memory lane.

Do something they love, that they know you don't. And if you don't enjoy it don't complain. Let them enjoy themselves.

Write a note. Boring? Not at all. Tell your man how sexy he is, with an invitation, and put it in his underwear when he is asleep. He'll be more surprised to find it in a surprising place!

Make his day with some surprise lingerie. Or whatever outfit he thinks is super sexy. Wait for him in the bedroom. Or wear nothing at all.

You know what they like. C'mon put your thinking cap on and surprise your loved one.

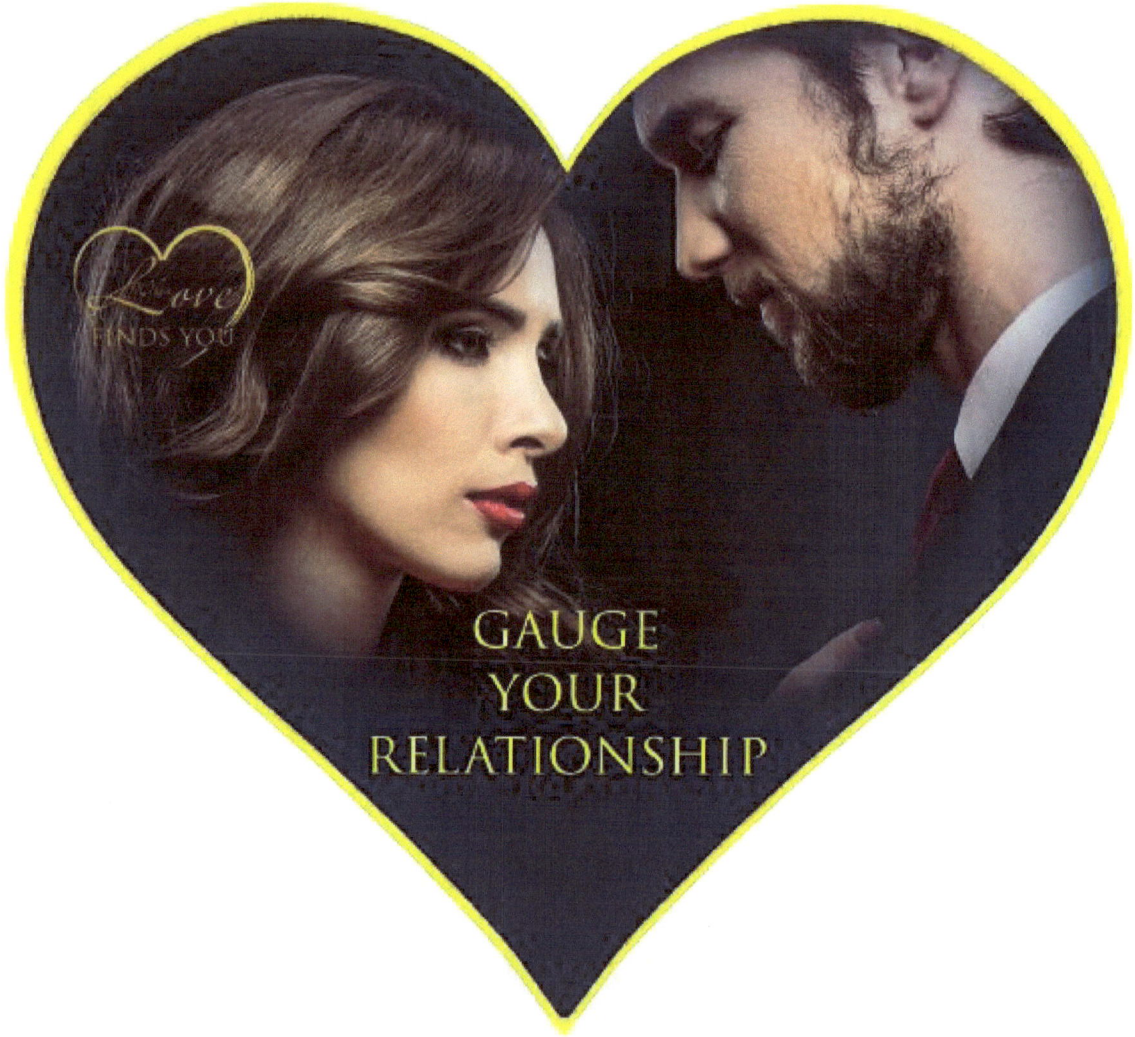

Love FINDS YOU

GAUGE
YOUR
RELATIONSHIP

On a scale of 1–10 rate the current state of your marriage or relationship today. One means on the verge of divorce—poor communication, no intimacy. Ten is the dream marriage, however you picture that to be.

Six means average. Not great but not bad. If it's in a static place (also called a rut), beware of the slippery slope!

Try these exercises to raise the needle on the scale!

When she has had a super-stressful day or a happy one—listen. Don't give advice. Let her talk. Truly listen. Repeat back to her succinctly what you heard, what happened and how she felt. Confirm 'Do I have it right?' with empathy. She will feel heard and understood and that is a powerful thing.

Tell him that you are looking forward to tonight. It will pique his interest. He will feel excited and appreciated. When the kids go to bed, tell him you are taking the time to celebrate 'Us'. Look through your wedding album, talk—really talk. Let the evening take you where it will.

Love is a Verb. Something you DO.

LOVE FINDS YOU

BRIGHTEN
EACH
OTHERS
DAY

The best romantic partners somehow know just how to brighten your day. They understand you don't need some grand gesture. A simple note, a tight hug or a favourite meal can brighten a cloudy day. When they feel better, you feel better.

Write notes that consist of sweet affirmations, an inside joke, a special word or a thoughtful reminder.

Sometimes all they need is reassuring comments and arms around them to make them feel like everything is okay.

Give your partner a funny card to make them laugh when they don't feel like laughing.

Shoot them a silly text to make them smile.

Get goofy with them.

Bring her dinner in bed. There are not many things that a grilled cheese sandwich on a heart-shaped plate made by your man can't fix.

Find opportunities to squeeze, hug, rub, nuzzle, cuddle, or hold your partner throughout the day in a non-sexual way.

Kiss them on the cheek while they're sorting the mail.

Gently rub her feet when she's watching Netflix.

Rest your hand on his knee when you're sitting next to each other in the car.

You get the idea.

SET
GROUND
RULES

All couples fight. But … there is an art to arguing. It's the way couples argue that determines if their relationship will go the distance. Happy couples colour inside the lines.

Pour a glass of wine and set some ground rules, when you are both in a good space.

Agree not to shy away from topics that could easily be swept under the rug. When are we going to have kids? Buy a house?

Agree to be respectful. It's fine to say 'I'm furious right now'. Not fine to say ' You are a poor excuse for a human being'.

Agree to address the issue softly. Argue with finesse. One person speaks and the other truly listens.

Definitely agree to no name-calling, eye-rolling or biting sarcasm.

If things get out of hand, agree to take time out. Don't forget you are a team.

Agree to give your partner the benefit of the doubt. Don't assume your partner wants to jump ship because they are voicing their concerns.

Agree to disagree.

Keep the fights clean and the sex dirty!

ACCEPT
FLAWS

We love our special significant other. They are a source of happiness and comfort in our lives. However, as humans who possess special, unique traits, we can easily get annoyed with habits that don't fit our personality frames.

Tell him you hate his silly little habit of making a mess in the bathroom sink. But make sure you tell him that you appreciate his shoulder to lean on every time it is needed, without fail. What's a bit of toothpaste, after all?!

Acknowledge you get annoyed at her always leaving the car door unlocked. But accept that she is juggling kids and groceries and forgets most times. She is not doing it on purpose.

Tell him it annoys you when he rolls his eyes at you when you bicker over some triviality but acknowledge his extreme kindness and generosity. The day your dog died and he waited on you hand and foot, taking over all necessary arrangements, because you were a total mess.

At the end of the day, the essential, more significant things outweigh those annoying little imperfections.

Focus on what's right not wrong. You get it.

REMEMBER QUALITIES YOU LOVE

Remember the moments and reasons why your partner is special and important to you.
Get out that glass of wine when the kids have gone to bed. And remember …

He lets things roll off his back. He lets you be right.

He puts the kids to bed and handles night shift.

He's like the Pied Piper of Hamlin when it come to kids on the playground.

He runs errands and goes grocery shopping.

He can hold a conversation with anyone he meets.

He loves the kids to pieces.

He is tough and resilient, except when he is a softie.

Get the idea?

What does your man do that gives you that warm fuzzy feeling?

Tell him.

She is my best friend.

My partner is an amazing mother and parent.

She shows me I'm worthy to be loved.

I can't imagine life without her.

She never quits on herself, or us.

She whispers 'I love you' before falling asleep.

She rolls up the toothpaste tube for me.

She is your woman. Your life.

Let her know.

DAYDREAM
TOGETHER

Daydreams can change our mood—they can relax us and change the way we feel. They move us from our logical mind and thinking into our heart and feelings.

Daydreaming isn't a waste of time, as we're often told, but the gateway to creativity and problem solving, especially those persistent problems that keep coming up in our relationship. Set them aside for a while and indulge in daydreaming with your partner. It will be fun and help to connect with your partner.

Winning millions of dollars in the lottery is the ultimate daydream because nothing else would ever be as life-changing. Think about buying a ticket. Just one. You never know. What would you and your partner do with all that moola?

Fantasise about leaving your jobs, selling all your possessions and travelling the world together … till the money runs out and you have to return to the grind. What would you do on your adventure?

Engaging in constructive sexual fantasies can help a relationship! Check out the 'Explore Sexual Fantasies' card for some ideas. If consensual, get moving!

Dream together. Feel good.

JUST
a
DREAM

EXPLORE
SEXUAL
FANTASIES

Love
FINDS YOU

Being able to communicate your desires to your partner, keeping things new, and adding imagination to sex will do wonders for you both. Remember consensus.
Here are some sizzling sexcapades—do you dare?!

VOYEURISM

Does watching the show from the sidelines turn you on? Go to a nude beach or a sex show with your partner.

ACT OUT YOUR FAVOURITE SEX SCENE FROM A MOVIE.

Get into character and re-create your favourite cinematic sex scene. Discuss the scene with your partner and get ready for an Academy Award-winning performance.

MAKE A SEX VIDEO

Make a homemade flick with your partner. After you watch it make sure to hide it safely or delete it.

OUTDOOR SEX

Try it in a secluded area outside at night. The grass, the pool, the great outdoors is your sex playground.

MUTUAL MASTURBATION

Put a twist on your voyeuristic fantasy. Watching your partner masturbate or letting him watch you. An instant turn on.

PUT ON A STRIP SHOW

Put on your sexiest lingerie, take it off and tease him in the process, private lap dance included.

SCHEDULE SEX

Once the honeymoon period dies down, things in the sex department simmer down too. But it shouldn't fall off a cliff!

Children take up a lot of time and effort. Sex is an activity that seems to be last on the list. Putting sex on the calendar may seem unromantic and boring. But scheduling sex can still be romantic and fun.

Talk about the fact that both of you have busy schedules, and that scheduling sex can guarantee there is enough time for intimacy. Don't make it too official.

Agree that you'll go to bed early on a Friday night. You can watch some fun movies together, and then spend some intimate time together in bed.

Schedule some time together on Sunday afternoons. The kids can go to grandma's for lunch.

Schedule a couple of minutes on Monday morning—just for a quickie. Great start to the new week!

You have your own agenda. Pencil your appointments into the calendar and keep them!

Don't stop doing the deed. There's no excuse for ever losing that spark!

COMPLIMENT EACH OTHER

No matter where you are in your relationship, a few months or thirty years, everyone needs to be loved or desired.

It's time you complimented them on those things you love. How else will they ever know?

Here are a few authentic compliments to pay your partner. Often and always.

I love the way you make me feel: This is short and full of meaning.

There's no one else like you: That says you love their individuality.

You're such a good …

Whatever your partner is good at, let them know. 'You're such a good cook.' 'You're such a good mum.'

I love the way your mind works.

When your partner has just expressed a new thought or done something creative or you just feel inspired, let them know you love the way their mind works.

You're the love of my life.

No one can hear this enough.

You are my world.

Being someone's world? One of the highest compliments you can give.

Remind them of how special they are to you. Shout it from the rooftops.

Love

HAVE A ROMANTIC PICNIC

A picnic can be a wonderful romantic tryst. Plan an Afternoon Delight Picnic.

Parks, gardens, an open meadow, wooded areas, on a hillside with a view of the valley, beside water—rivers, lakes or waterfalls are all good picnic spots.

When you have a day off, get him to take the afternoon off work with some fake believable excuse.

Prepare the picnic surprise when he has left for work.

Get an old school picnic basket. Yes, old fashioned to make it as romantic as possible. Use real cutlery,

plates and champagne glasses. Don't forget the champers! Prepare a romantic menu.

Strawberries should never be missing in a romantic picnic. Meat and veggies, pickles, sauces, sandwiches, and other gourmet goodies. The best dark chocolate—yum!

A special blanket to lie on, not something itchy and common that everyone has.

Dress up old school with a long flowing dress and sunhat. Romantic music and your partner's favourite dessert, along with candles and flowers, complete the ideal picnic set up.

Pick him up from work and whisper sweet nothings in his ear while he sips champagne.

The two of you will head home to an afternoon of sensual delights.

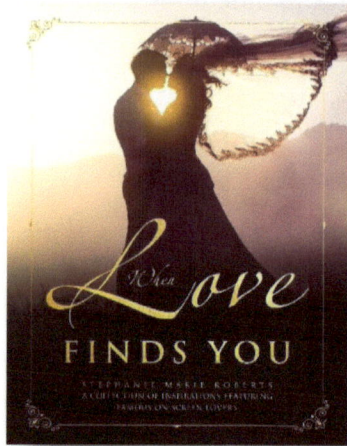

EBook on Amazon

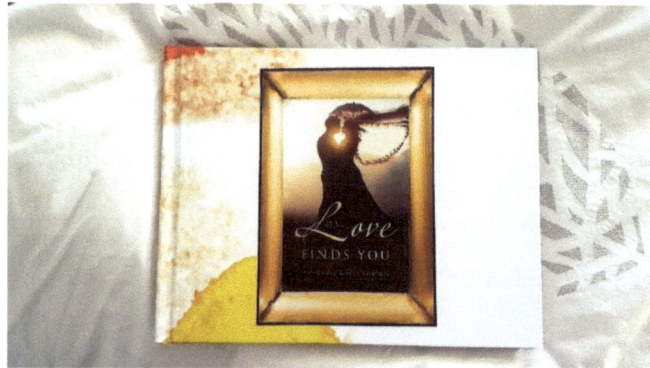

Coffee Table Hardcover Book available from website:

https://stephaniemarieroberts.com

STEPHANIE MARIE ROBERTS
A COLLECTION OF INSPIRATIONS FEATURING FAMOUS ON-SCREEN LOVERS

A lot of people don't understand what real romance is.

The true romantic things in life are those little everyday gestures to show your loved one you care. Bringing her a cup of tea in bed when she wakes up in the morning. Being there for her when she is troubled and scared, even if it is because the dog is spewing from eating all the sausages and she is worried he is going to die that day. Putting your footy show on pause to listen to her narrative about her day. Texting or phoning her from work just to say, 'I love you', because you thought of her.

Romance isn't all about buying gifts and flowers. It's about the doing and caring. The little things you do every day to show you care. They are the big things ♡.

ABOUT THE AUTHOR

Stephanie Marie Roberts writes children's books and romance. She is a Book Excellence Literary Award Winner and Silver Medallist for *Joshua's World* and *Liam Shark Boy*. She started writing for her little grandsons Joshua and Liam, which grew into writing for all the kids of the world!

Stephanie is also an incurable romantic. She was born in India in post Second World War days when children were seen but not heard, to parents of Anglo-Indian origin. Her father served as a dive bomber and fighter pilot in the India and Burma theatres of war during the Second World War. She has just released a heart-warming historic romance novel *Always* based on true incidents from her life.

Two beautifully illustrated books: a coffee table book of inspirations *When Love Finds You* and her heart book *The Well of True Gestures* helps couples bond in their relationship.

Stephanie lives on the beautiful Central Coast of Australia with her retired secret-service husband Chris and sixteen-year-old pampered Cocker Spaniel Harvey. Dogs are her passion and she must have a dog under her feet when she writes.

For Hardcover coffee table version or any other paperbacks not available on Amazon, write to stephanieroberts@iinet.net.au to order direct.

Website:

https://stephaniemarieroberts.com

Facebook Author Pages:

Romance: https://www.facebook.com/StephanieRobertsAuthor/

Kids: https://www.facebook.com/StephanieRobertsWriter/

www.ingramcontent.com/pod-product-compliance
Lightning Source LLC
Chambersburg PA
CBHW060822270326

41931CB00002B/54